Fatma Karoui

The evolution of the weaving activity

AF376113

Fatma Karoui

The evolution of the weaving activity

Transition of weaving from a traditional domestic auxiliary activity to a new production for the market

ScienciaScripts

Imprint
Any brand names and product names mentioned in this book are subject to trademark, brand or patent protection and are trademarks or registered trademarks of their respective holders. The use of brand names, product names, common names, trade names, product descriptions etc. even without a particular marking in this work is in no way to be construed to mean that such names may be regarded as unrestricted in respect of trademark and brand protection legislation and could thus be used by anyone.

Cover image: www.ingimage.com

This book is a translation from the original published under ISBN 978-620-2-54135-0.

Publisher:
Sciencia Scripts
is a trademark of
International Book Market Service Ltd., member of OmniScriptum Publishing Group
17 Meldrum Street, Beau Bassin 71504, Mauritius
Printed at: see last page
ISBN: 978-620-2-83855-9

Copyright © Fatma Karoui
Copyright © 2020 International Book Market Service Ltd., member of OmniScriptum Publishing Group

THE CARPET WEAVING FROM THE DOMESTIC ACTIVITY OF AUXILIARY DOMESTIC ACTIVITY TO AN ORGANIZED MARKET PRODUCTION.

SUMMARY

INTRODUCTION

Kairouan presents a field of investigation and analysis given the importance of the practice of weaving. The carpet represents one of the riches of the city of Kairouan. It was and remains until today a specificity and a characteristic of the city elevated to the rank of national heritage because it translates since its creation, a whole culture.

It is indeed a particular work of art which reveals by its drawings and colors and the material used a whole tradition specific to the city, created by Kairouanese women.

Woman, wool, colors and patterns are intertwined. What is the origin of this link and how was it created? What are the materials used and their origins?

The carpet is considered as a heritage product that affects both the material heritage: the product from which it is made or woven and the support on which it is woven. And the intangible heritage: the way of preparing the wool, the dyeing and the weaving itself.

The common point between these two components is the woman; she is the one who is at the base of the manufacturing of this heritage product from the raw material to its realization.

Such a study aims at the knowledge of the historical stages of the assertion of this know-how, the reconstitution of a historical collection and the valorization of this heritage product sign of the identity of this city. It will have the merit of preserving a heritage craft that is under threat.

At the same time, this research proposes a study of the stakeholders who are the markers of the manufacture of this product and the process, to highlight women's work throughout history and whose museumization is necessary for the preservation of this female heritage.

Weaving is the ancestral female domestic activity par excellence. It has undergone several changes through the various historical stages and conjunctures that the country has known. After independence and with the promulgation of the

Personal Status Code, women acquired broad socio-economic rights. Thus, "the number of jobs held by women in non-agricultural sectors increased fivefold between 1956 and 1975, from a little over 40,000 to nearly 203,000[1].

Indeed, since independence Tunisia has undergone various changes that have affected political, social, economic and cultural life. All these transformations are essentially the consequence of policies of societal modernization in both urban and rural areas.

A new legislation for the benefit of women, which gave them a new status, both at the personal and social level, consolidated this modernization and this by the promulgation in August 1956, the Personal Status Code. These new jurisdictions will have important repercussions on the status of Tunisian women and on family structures. They contributed to the improvement of social relations and roles by facilitating women's access to the labor market and their recognition as economic actors, which is essential for the country's development.

Within the framework of the first development plans, based on a socializing economic policy, the state encouraged profitable economic investments. The hotel and tourism sectors presented opportunities for craft activity.

The manufacturing industries were located mainly on the coast, where women's weaving occupies an important place in the socio-economic development of the country.

To this end, and with the contribution of several governmental and non-governmental stakeholders, has worked for the evolution and promotion of crafts, which has proved to be a very promising sector for development. Among these operators, we note the National Handicrafts Office, the training centers for rural girls under development programs and the Union of Tunisian Women.

This is what prompted us to carry out this work, in order to list the traditions of craft work especially the Kairouan Carpet, to identify and study the different transformations and evolutions in women's weaving, whose main mutation is that of its transition from a traditional domestic activity to a new production intended for the

---

[1] S. Bessis, S. Belhassen, *Femmes du Maghreb : l'enjeu, Tunis,* Cérès Production, 1992, p :82.

market. On the other hand, we will try to understand the impact of this evolution on the life and status of women artisans, and to know the fate of this endangered cultural heritage.

I. <u>Weavers' stories and routes :</u>

I have chosen the testimonies of these working women, among several, to analyze their situation, since each one has lived an interesting and unique experience.

1- <u>ZOHRA AYARI</u>: salaried weaver "an exceptional weaver".

She is another weaver of Kairouanese origin, 66 years old, in love with her profession and ready to do everything to keep it. This is how she testified:

"I didn't *finish high school, I started weaving at the age of 16. I followed in the footsteps of my mother Mabrouka Mejri who taught me the weaving craft, I wanted to imitate her and learn a trade; carpet weaving because I like this job very much. This is how I have been doing it for 50 years and with a lot of passion. I work with great pleasure and with a lot of motivation and enthusiasm.*

I started to learn weaving around the fifties, I was 16 years old, at that time I could easily master the weaving techniques with the help of my mother. Then I started to make these weavings by myself and I sold them in the souk. Even after my marriage I continued to work at home to help my husband improve the family's financial situation. After my divorce and with 5 children I was forced to work to support my children.

So I started to work with a fixed salary in a handicraft until today and this for more than 36 years. At the same time, I have kept my weaving tool, which is made of wood, at home and after work, when I come home and depending on my condition, I make a few knots or lines ".

And she added: "*Kairouanese women are active and productive and I can't sit idle, without any work, I am always looking for ways to improve my living conditions. So I continued to work in this craft which is located in the tourist circuit so that tourists can observe the weaving technique and I supervise other weavers who work with me.*

I also supervise the quality of the woven carpets. And sometimes, if necessary, I make interventions at the level of the proposed scheme to improve it.

For the sale and the exhibition of the carpet in the store it is the person in charge who takes care of it, his role is limited to the reception of the customers and the presentation of the different types of carpets. I have also participated in several national and international exhibitions of craftsmanship with the sole purpose of making this craft known ".

As for the homemade carpet: "*I take care of it and I go to the carpet souk to sell it. And the money that I earn is primarily for the purchase of wool and the rest for the needs of the family and the house. As for creating my own project, I consider it very difficult at the moment because I can't create a weaving workshop on my own; it requires a big investment and total availability. On top of that, the market is dominated by the big traders and the intermediaries of the carpet, and already I find it very difficult to sell my work directly and I must necessarily go through these intermediaries who monopolize the market. In addition, there are social and family constraints, since in our society men do not accept that their wives, daughters or mothers rub shoulders with men or traders in the souk. In addition to these constraints, many women stop weaving after marriage, as it is a tiring job that absorbs time and affects women's health, especially with the heavy load they assume between household chores and child rearing, especially since men do not participate in any of these tasks.*

She continued: "*The carpet market today is in decline, the prices of carpets are very high due to the increase in the price of wool and also of labor and on top of that there is no more demand as before. To sell a carpet it is necessary to pay several commissions; that of the middleman, that of the one who exposes the carpet for the customer and the worker finally receives only a small sum which allows him hardly to repay his debts and buy the wool again. And another very important stage, that of the stamping which will determine the price of the carpet according to whether it is stamped first or second choice which can lead to a sale below the cost price. She added: "There are several weaving workshops today that are spread over several areas, which are not declared and which suffer financially, because customers, mostly tourists, are becoming increasingly scarce. Tunisians no longer buy these traditional carpets, given their price, and in addition they prefer industrialized carpets, which are obviously much cheaper and widespread on the market.*

After all these years of weaving, I don't intend to change my job, despite the low salary I receive from my boss, because I'm going to take a big risk by creating my own project, as the sector is not as flourishing as it used to be".

Finally, she confided to me: "*I am sick at heart to see this craft disappearing over time and if I had the power, I would make a revolution so that the people in charge take better care of this craft and the women who work there to encourage them to give their best and not get tired of it and then I would look for another more profitable job that would allow them to live better*" before asserting: "I don't *intend to stop my work, I want to keep continuity, besides, this loom represents the air I breathe and I can't go a day without tying a knot or passing a weft thread and my weaving tool is like a sacred object that I can't take out of the house*".

Illustration n°35 : Mrs. Zohra Ayri weaving a carpet.

2- MAHBOUBA WESLATI : salaried weaver

This weaver does not look like other weavers

"I am 69 years old, born in Kairouan and belong to a large rural family. I didn't finish my primary education and it is for material needs that I learned to weave and of course with the encouragement of my family.

It is Mrs. Zohra known by "El Mestiria" a patroness, who taught me weaving and with whom I continued to work. I was paid according to the number of lines woven; a very small sum.

Divorced for 30 years, I have four children and have been working since the age of 15. It has been almost 15 years since I started working with Mrs. ZOHRA AYARI in the handicraft industry where I had a fixed salary. And nowadays, my eyes hurt and I can't see well, but in spite of that I continue to work, not out of love for my job, but out of need of money I have to feed my children. And since I don't have an association that defends me and helps me to have a minimum that will allow me to rest after a long career of 50 years, and which even reaches 60 and 65 years of work for some of them since they start at the age of 10 to 15, they find themselves obliged to work despite their poor physical condition to provide for themselves and their children".

She spoke with much bitterness, unlike her colleague Mrs. Zohra Ayari, whose testimony was just presented.

3- ESSIA ALLANI : weaver at home " of a well-to-do family ".

She is a 91 year old woman, known for her good mood,

"I am 94 years old, of Kairouanese origin and a widow with three children. I started weaving at the age of six in my father's home and it was my mother who taught me the craft since it was a tradition in all families; a young girl must learn to weave, not for material reasons but out of love for this noble craft. And since this age I did not stop working on the carpet, I even made a large carpet to offer it to the tomb of "Sidi Sahbi" as any young girl of that time, then I prepared the carpets of my wedding trousseau, with different types and sizes.

Even after my marriage, the loom I was working on was still installed in the house. During the day, I managed to divide my time between the children, cooking and weaving. And it was only in the evening, after the children were asleep, that I took care of myself and my well being before my husband returned home:

"With experience, I ended up working without a model to follow, it was habit and know-how that guided me in my weaving. I sold my carpets at home for individuals who knew my work and who came to buy with confidence and this lasted between forty and fifty long years. And of course, with the money I earned, I bought, first of all, wool to be able to start another carpet and the rest was for the renovation of my furniture or utensils or for the purchase of my daughters' wedding trousseaux. And at the same time I taught the girls and the neighbors the weaving techniques. And I can proudly say that many young girls learned weaving thanks to me".

And finally she assured me: "I am satisfied and even happy with the career I have led, especially having taught several young girls the weaving profession. I am also happy because I exercised my passion without constraints, I was my own boss and I didn't encounter any problems throughout my career since I worked when I wanted to since I didn't have any money problems".

illustration n°38: Mrs. Essya Allani during the interview, 93 years old.

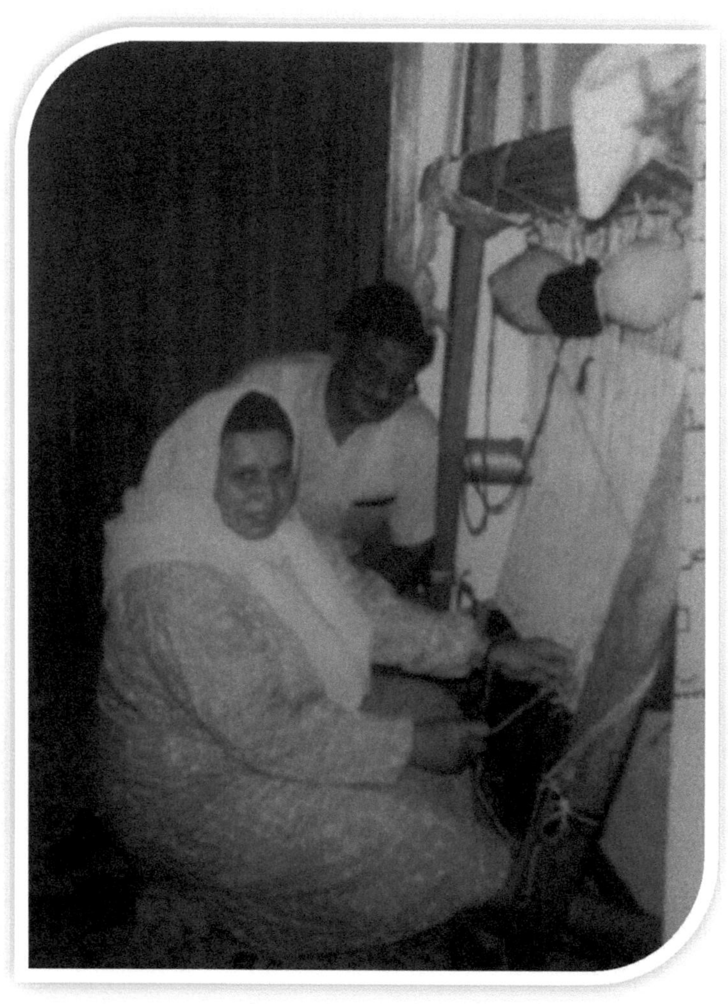

Illustration n°39: Mrs. Essya Allani weaving a carpet in the 70s.

4- Fathia Akoub: weaver boss with her own project

"I am 57 years old, a widow and mother of 4 children, originally from Kairouan. I come from a modest family. I didn't finish primary school, as my father didn't see the importance of education. At the age of eleven or twelve we left school and had to stay at home to learn an activity. At that time, I saw my father working day and night to support us, my mother didn't work, she didn't even do weaving, which was a common activity among Kairouanese women. But she was not interested in weaving (or any other activity), apart from housework, she did nothing. At that time, when I was 12 years old, I saw my paternal aunts who all did weaving and baking to help their husbands and improve their standard of living.

And from there, I decided to help my father by learning how to weave. I went every day to my aunt's house to learn the weaving techniques and I worked with her and every time she sold a carpet she would give me my share, I put away this money until the day came when I decided to buy my own loom with the money I earned. It was the great joy and the beginning of the realization of my dreams.

I set up my loom in my room, it was and still is my great passion, I spent a whole day weaving without getting bored, and at the end of each carpet, it was party time at home. I would sell my carpet at the souk, after having it stamped, and I would go to my aunt's house to make a tray of "Baklawa", with the ingredients I bought with my own money, and then I would take it home as a gift for my parents and brothers.

I love my job and I worked it with great patience. After I got married, my job was even easier and my work path was almost clear, as my husband was a "*Hedgek*" weaver on a low loom. My husband helped me a lot in buying wool and selling carpets. So I set up on my own, I worked in my house at the beginning, and little by little my project expanded and I set up a garage that I rented, and I recruited morning girls to work with me. Apart from weaving, I was doing embroidery on the "Hayek" that my husband was making.

Thanks to the work of weaving, in the seventies   my husband and I were able to buy a piece of land and then we built our house together. Even with the children, I didn't find any problems, my day was well organized. But at that time we didn't think about the future or what might happen in the future, we lived from day to day without worrying about tomorrow.

With the sudden death of my husband, I first felt that everything had stopped and that I could no longer continue on my own. But, after some time, I had to resume my work and my husband's work at the same time. I reopened my workshop in which I had about twenty young weavers working, they were paid according to the number of lines woven. At that   time, there was a great demand for Kairouanese carpets. Nowadays, we have few customers.

The problem also appears with the morning girls, they no longer want to work in weaving, they prefer to work in a factory, or as a worker with their face hidden for fear that they will not be recognized. While the salary is the same; a matinee earns from 150 Dinard to 200 Dinard per month with good conditions.

Another major problem in this business is the marketing of the product. Indeed, the flow of goods is the prerogative of the "dallals" and the big traders, who monopolize the whole carpet souk. These middlemen take a percentage of the price of the carpet. Even if I want to market my production on my own, I can't, because traders and middlemen are organized in networks and monopolize the market. Thus, tourists are intercepted as soon as they enter the souk and "led" directly to the handicraft stores in the medina, to these same merchants who   give a commission in return. Thus, the craftswomen cannot directly access the customers. It is only through these intermediaries and these "dallals" that they can sell their production.

She paused for a moment laughing and then continued by saying, "I'll tell you an anecdote. One day, while I was working in my weaving shop, one of the "baznessa" came with a tourist who wanted to buy an average carpet and asked me the price, and I answered that I wanted one thousand two hundred for myself and that he could add his commission. The latter, believing that I didn't understand French, asked the customer for three thousand dinars! And there I was flabbergasted. Yet I was the one who had to pay the weavers to buy the wool and then get my share and he dared to inflate the price so much!   I then asked for another price and I threatened him, if he did not agree to deal directly with the tourist. »

And she went on to say:

"Fortunately, I sometimes get orders through relatives and friends, who live abroad, who order carpets from me for customers abroad. Or through people who know me personally and who give me word-of-mouth advertising. I also participate in several national and international fairs with my own productions.

However, this type of marketing is not common and has its limits. Sometimes I go through moments of crisis when I can only sell my production by selling at low prices. This is a necessary sacrifice if I don't want to stop working, continue paying the weavers and pay off my debts. In spite of these constraints, I am satisfied with my professional career, I attend seminars and training courses organized by the civil society. I also attend seminars organized by the state in order to improve the working conditions of the weavers, as their number is rapidly decreasing. I also try to find ways to   market my creations and productions abroad, so through export, I can help in the economic growth of the country. »

5- <u>The problems encountered by the weavers through their testimonies :</u>

The work of weaving requires a lot of patience[2] and endurance because these women spend days and nights weaving.

One often hears it said in the weaver's entourage: "*Poor thing, she spent her whole life working on the carpet, and as she gets older she needs someone to take care of her. "The weaving* work is considered to be exhausting for the health, indeed the development of the loom is a tiring work requiring the intervention of several individuals at the same time because the warp beams are very heavy and require a great precision.

Apart from the installation of the loom, which is usually done in one day, the weaver sits for hours, days and even months in front of her loom to finalize her work. She usually sits on a low stool or on a klim on the floor, and in these two positions she has her back bent, her feet crossed and her hands suspended which make successive and regular knots like a machine work, and she must have her eyes fixed on the warp threads which are numerous and intertwined[3]. Then, after several lines she takes the cup which is made of solid iron, therefore heavy enough to pack the woven lines. So at the end of the day, or after several hours of continuous work she finds herself stiff, her feet heavy and her hands and back stuck. And despite the fatigue, as soon as she regains her strength, she starts working on other tasks around the house.

We can conclude that the weavers during all their day are forced to keep painful attitudes which prove to deform their limbs and which often make them contract infirmities. These women are fighters.

There are some women who suffer from this work but have no choice, it is the only way to survive. Mrs. **MAHBOUBA WESLATI**, 69 years old, divorced for 30 years, with 4 children, started working at the age of 15. This woman does not

---

[2]Nacer, Baklout, *op. cit.* p. 7. "Spinner or weaver, the woman spends hours manipulating spindle and distaff or tying stitches around the warp threads, without tiring, reproducing repetitive and eternal gestures, chanted by mnemonic songs transmitted from mother to daughter".

[3] Jacques, Revault, *op. cit,* p.18. "Sitting on a mat or a sheepskin, the weaver does not suffer from the tiring position that the loom of the basse lisse inflicts on her. »

resemble the two others already mentioned because it is for material needs that she learned weaving and of course with the encouragement of her family. It is a patroness Mrs. Zohra known by "el mestiria", who taught her weaving and with whom she continued to work. She was paid according to the number of lines woven; a very small sum. Almost 15 years ago she started to work with Mrs. Zohra Ayari in the handicraft industry where she received a fixed salary. And today, her eyes hurt and she can no longer see well, but in spite of this she continues to work, not out of love for her, but out of necessity; to feed herself and her children. And since the weavers don't have an organization that defends them and helps them to obtain a small pension, even a small one to allow them to rest after a long career of 50 years, and that even reaches 60 and 65 years of work, since they start at the age of 10 and 15 and they are forced to work despite their precarious physical condition.

These weavers also suffer from poor remuneration. Nowadays, the cost of wool keeps rising and it is no longer profitable. Because the weaver earns very little on carpets. The profits go to the middlemen. For a square meter of margoum or carpet, the weaver earns very little while the selling price is double and sometimes even triple. Of course, prices vary and increase over time from the fifties to the present day. To have an idea of the magnitude of the task, know that the creation of a Kairouanese carpet of 6 meters high by 4 meters wide requires 4 women and 22 days of work at least and it can go up to a month.

Mrs. Halima, 55 years old, spoke of her mother's suffering and fatigue with great bitterness. Since her father has no stable job, her mother is forced to work to feed her children. She would get up very early in the morning to work in the fields, and with the money she earned she would buy every Wednesday unclean woollen cloth, which she had at home, carded, painted and finally spun, in order to be able to sell it the following Wednesday in the wool souk, otherwise she would have to wait until the following Wednesday. Then she learned weaving from her neighbor and with the wool work she was able to buy a loom and she started making carpets and selling them. At the age of 14, Mrs. Halima decided to help her mother, whom she had always seen tired, she stopped her studies and started to work in a factory as a weaver. After her marriage, she started to work at home on her own loom and since then, she only weaves carpets but of course her performance is not the same today.

She has health problems because of her crouching in front of her loom, and the selling price is no longer profitable.

The stamping stage is also an important but stressful step for the weavers. Because after a month of work and fatigue, the weaver has to stand in line on Wednesday, the only stamping day, to stamp her carpet and be able to sell it in the souk, otherwise it will not be sold. After this step she takes her carpet to the "***Errbaa***" carpet souk to sell it by auction. And with this money she barely manages to pay back her debts, to buy the wool for a new carpet and to have some pocket money for herself.

In spite of the pain these women feel, during the interview they all say the same thing: "*I love the work of weaving and I can no longer part with my loom, it is always present in the house as if it were a member of the family. Even if I am tired or sick I do a few lines during the day, because the work of weaving becomes like a compulsory and necessary ritual during the day.* »

In recounting their journey, the weavers proudly explained that they have chosen to make carpet weaving their profession because for them, this ancestral heritage is very valuable. A Kairouanese carpet leaves an imprint long after its creator has passed away. It is a way of living still through his creations beyond death.

Habib Ben Mansour spoke of the importance of craftswomen in the conservation and passing on of an ancestral heritage" There was in this city of Kairouan a real technical tradition, a mastery of the art of weaving that many craftswomen have testified. Spinners, dyers and weavers had long since established the reputation of Kairouan and will constitute the human fabric, the fertile ground on which the evolution of the carpet will unfold[4].

a- <u>Sabbahat" mornings</u>

Sabbahat are the weavers who work under the direction of a "Maalma" boss. They are so called because they start their work at dawn. Their work is very hard because generally these weavers are forced to weave, not out of love for the loom, but out of necessity, especially since they cannot afford to buy a loom. According to

---

[4] Habib Ben Mansour, *op. cit,* P: 30

the testimony of some weavers, they start the apprenticeship very early since the age of 14 with a "Maalma", most of them are not from Kairouan city, they come from the surrounding villages to help their families. Then, after their marriage, they find themselves obliged to work to support their families as well.

Every boss has a space, usually near or juxtaposed to her house, it's a bare-walled garage where there are installed, looms juxtaposed, with just a lamp hanging from the ceiling. The weavers sit next to each other, facing the back wall in front of their wooden looms. Behind them is another row of weavers.

illustration n°38[5] : Sabbahat weaving a carpet at "Dar Maalma".

---

[5]Hedia, Baraket, *femmes du bout des doigts, " Kairouan: " les matinales " se réveiller ailleurs,* CREDIF 1995, p: 21.

One of the travelers, during his visit to Kairouan "Joan Roig" described several types of carpets and he stressed that "the weavers have a life of misery, that they work a high number of hours in the day, in a small dark workshop full of cobwebs[6].

These women are paid according to the number of rows, according to Mrs. Fathia Akoub, boss, she pays the 30 rows at six dinars that the weaver finishes in one morning; so per month they earn 150 dinars and of course they have no social security coverage. "They are the "matinales", workers paid on a piecework basis, so called because they work in the morning and only in the morning. In the habits and customs of the trade, this is the precious and laborious moment, which contrasts sharply with idle afternoons".[7]

At dawn, the weavers begin their work, sitting on wooden benches or on rush bags filled with wool waste. Some of them prefer to work for a boss rather than on their own account to guarantee a fixed daily wage, except for a few times when they are paid in advance or after the sale of the carpet, and for this reason they may change from one workshop to another.

By working for a "*Maalma*", on the one hand the weaver will guarantee a fixed and regular remuneration, even if it is low, and on the other hand she saves herself the procedure of stamping.

b- Stamping and marketing

It is the mark of quality that sticks to the back of the carpet and takes into consideration, besides the quality of the raw materials used, the artistic and physical aspects as well as the technical specifications of the finished product. Refusal or rejection for production stamping is therefore justified by non-compliance and non-compliance with the agreed standards.

---

[6] José Luis Villanova, IBLA "Kairouan and Spanish tourists, 2012, p.27.
[7] Hedia, Baraket, op.cit., p: 21.

➢ **Stamping steps :**

The steps required for stamping are :

-Ensure the receipt or invoice for the purchase of the raw material to guarantee the conformity of the wool used with what is requested.

-Check the weight.

- Control the texture.

- Control the organization and the border.

- Control the quality of the color of the wool used.

- Check the curl of the carpet.

- Control the technical qualities of the wool (categories and modes of use).

➢ **The standardization of carpet stamping :**

The standardization of the manufacture of carpets and weavings and the classification of the finished product is dictated by the economic and social importance of this artisanal activity at the national level.

The manufacturing standards for carpets and short weavings gathered in this collection imposed by usage and tradition have been adopted by the ONA and the INNORPI (National Institute of Standardization and Industrial Property).

These standards specify the raw materials used in production and determine the qualities attributed to the finished product by the stamping assigned to ONA.

Tapisserie

Les matières premières utilisées dans la fabrication de la tapisserie sont la laine et le coton.

SPECIFICATIONS TECHNIQUES DE LA MATIERE

Désignation	NATURE	Utilisation
Chaine	- Coton câblé 20 / 6 - Coton câblé 20 / 9 - Coton câblé 20 / 12	
T R A M E	Laine de couleur naturelle ou teinte : - Filée mécaniquement - Cardée, semi-peignée et peignée - Lavée, dégraissée et traitée à l'antimite. - Teinture solide à la lumière au lavage et au frottement.	

SPECIFICATIONS DU PRODUIT FINI ET CLASSIFICATION

Critères	Supérieur	1ème Choix	2ème Choix
Ourdissage	650 fils de chaine au mètre linéaire avec le 20 / 6 - 600 fils de chaine au mètre linéaire avec le 20 / 9 - 500 fils de chaine au mètre linéaire avec le 20 / 12	650fils de chaine au mètre linéaire avec le 20 / 6 - 600 fils de chaine au mètre linéaire avec le 20 / 9 - 500 fils de chaine au mètre linéaire avec le 20 / 12	600 fils dechaine au mètre linéaire avec le 20/ 6 -500 fils de chaine au mètre linéaire avec le 20/9 -400 fils de chaine au mètre linéaire avec le 20/12
Fils de chaine	Non apparent	Non apparent	Plus au moins apparent.
Poids	Mini. : 1,000 kg Maxi. : 1,600 kg	Mini.:1.000kg Maxi. : 1.600Kg	Mini.: 1,000kg Maxi.: 1,600kg
Coûtures des fentes	Ne dépassant pas 1 cm	Ne dépassant pas 5 cm	Ne dépassant pas 10 cm
Equerrage	Tolérance de 1%	Tolérance de1,5%.	Tolérance de 2%
Lisières	Régularité parfaite -Tissage double des lisières	Régularité et tissage double des lisières	- Irrégularité ne nuisant pas à l'aspect de la tapisserie.
Changement de ton	Néant	Néant	Léger dans le fond ou le décor et ne nuisant pas à l'aspect de la tapisserie.
Gondolage	Néant	Néant	Partiel ne nuisant pas à l'aspect de la tapisserie.
Opérations de finition	Brossage et repassage sur la face	Brossage et repassage sur la face	Brossage et repassage sur la face

Illustration n°39: Example of a collection of stamping standards

Thus, domestic or organized production benefits from the assistance of the public authorities and is subject to the State's quality label. A leaded label on the back of the carpet bears indications on the quality, texture, measurements, model, range and date of manufacture of the carpet.

Illustration n°40 : Quality label

> ## History :

As early as 1921, the Tunisian Arts Office instituted a state mark intended to be affixed on "traditional carpets, hand woven with wools colored by means of products of great dyeing". (Decree of August 10, 1921, Official Gazette of 17 / 8 / 1921). The domestic industry was thus increasingly guided, controlled and encouraged, and the frequent exhibitions contributed to form the taste of the public, as well as that of the producers.

With the promulgation of the Decree of March 25, 1936, the stamping evolved to impose more precise standards by being granted only to the carpets whose decoration corresponds strictly to the models and whose good texture was made of quality wool. J.Revault underlines that "since January 1st, 1937, the mark used is that of the Tunisian Office of Strandardisation (O.T.U.S) and its affixing had been entrusted to the Direction of Public Instruction by decree of January 29th, 1936"[8].

For some time, during the Protectorate, the carpets thus stamped were exempted, at their entry in France, from import duties and taxes. The manufacturing standards of the Kairouan zarbia, imposed by local customs and traditions, were then adopted and renewed by the ONA, instituting in its turn a quality label "tabâa" intended to guarantee the authenticity of origin and the quality of the wool, dyeing and texture of the carpets.

Domestic production, whether individual or organized in workshops, benefiting from the assistance of the public authorities represented today by the ONA and the INNORPI (National Institute for Standardization and Industrial Property) is thus compulsorily subjected to this quality label which adds commercial value to it, according to the 3 recognized choices: superior quality, 1st choice and 2nd choice. Stamping is a service granted free of charge by the Regional Delegations of Crafts. A label is stamped in a corner on the back of the carpet, it corresponds to the criteria of the granted choice and includes indications on the texture, the number of points per linear meter (ex: from 250 to 300 points, that is to say 90 000 points per m2), the quantity of raw materials (wool and cotton cabled 12/20), the dimensions, the weight (for a carpet 20/20, 1m2 weighs 3,200 to 3,500Kg), the model and the date of the stamping.

These selection criteria are also the subject of an official manual "Carpets and weavings. Norme d'Estampillage ", edited by the ONA. Finally, the stamping takes into account the qualities and technical standards, as well as the general, aesthetic and artistic aspect of the carpet.

The possible rejection to the production stamping is generally justified by the non respect and/or non conformity to the official standards. The carpets are declared not in conformity with the 1st choice if they do not respect the specificities of each type of texture and/or if they present one of the following defects:

The disgorgement of colors.

---

[8]Jaque Revault, *op. cit.,* p. 33.

The change of tone, in the background or in the decor.

The very noticeable irregularity of the cut and edges.

The visible warping on the work.

Tearing or puncturing in the carpet.

Before the establishment of this label, the weavers worked without any model or reference mark. Fleury continues "...the sober design as a whole is composed of few patterns but fortunately combined, it is eternal and unique for each family". This is what made it possible to pass on certain patterns from generation to generation.

If the executed model does not include colors, the craftswoman can mix the colors she wishes, otherwise she must reproduce them faithfully at the risk of being refused stamping or get only the 2nd choice. Today an unstamped piece is sold at a very low price, or even at a loss and the craftsman will not even be able to refund the purchase price of the raw materials and even less that of the labor.

In this extreme case, it will have to resort to loans if it can. It is a real situation of precariousness which settles for these craftswomen, with all the consequences on their daily life and by extension on the trade itself.

As for the carpets with floral motifs that are reserved for the trousseaux of the young Kairouanese brides, these are generally not stamped, because traditionally woven even before the engagement by the girl herself or by a close relative. It is the same for the carpets ordered by mutual agreement generally intended for a family use. All other carpets are submitted to the Stamping Service "Dar Et'tabaâ" in Kairouan where qualified stampers receive the weavers between 8 am and 11 am, according to the following schedule :

- Mondays, Wednesdays and Saturdays are reserved for   independent craftswomen.
- Thursday is reserved for workshop productions.
- On Tuesdays the stamping service moves to El Oueslatia.

Once the carpets are stamped, the women move to the SouqEr'rbaââ where the sale is made at the auction (d'lala). This sale takes place on the same days as the stamping, between 11 am and 1 pm and in the presence of craftswomen, intermediate traders, the Amine of the souq, the municipal town criers (dellela) and some curious people.

In 2007 for example, 20,150 carpets were stamped in Kairouan, including 12600 Zarbia produced by some 800 weavers. The remaining 7,500 pieces were distributed among the various other Kairouanese ras weavings, including mergoums.[9]

Today, the production locations have clearly differentiated themselves with the appearance of large production units. Thus, besides a few large companies exporting carpets, a large number of workshops (of about ten workers) are scattered in the rather popular districts of Kairouan, but especially in the surrounding towns and villages.

However, the carpet manufacturing remains an exclusivity for the workshops and the weavers working at home for their own account and even if some weavers of Kairouan still make the classic carpet without preconceived model, the use of the "tanqila" model is however tending to become generalized: the weavers looking for ease, prefer to work on "tanqila". Creation and improvisation then become a reflex. Indeed, from the same model, several carpets with different decorations can be woven according to the dexterity, taste and imagination of each craftswoman.

As for the marketing of the finished product which is done, as already described, most often through the traditional channel in the souk Er rbaâ where consumers but especially intermediate traders come, the price is set by the bidding (dlala). The second commercial circuit takes the path of the stores and bazaars of the city that supply the needs of tourists and also participate in part, in the export of Kairouanese carpet.

However, both shop-owners and intermediary traders complain about the lack of local, national or foreign demand for the product they want. These difficulties in the

---

[9] Information provided by the technical center for creation, innovation and maintenance of carpets

sale of this merchandise can only have a significant, even irreversible impact on the socio-economic situation of weavers in the first place and therefore on the entire sector of Tunisian handicrafts. This would cause a huge loss of income at all levels, both individual and national and would be responsible, in the more or less long term, for the disappearance of a jewel of the country's heritage know-how.

The stamping is done at the **national office of the craft industry**, once a week, every Wednesday, it is the last step to be done before the sale of the carpet which represents, for the weavers, a real test. We see them very early in the morning queuing in front of the office door which opens at eight o'clock in the morning, they are of all ages, those who live in Kairouan and others who come from the villages, with their carpets of different sizes and designs. They are all stressed, waiting for the result of the stamping: a stamp of the first or second choice.

Illustration n°41 : a weaver carrying her carpet for stamping

Controllers are picky, they notice that the morning work is not regular and uniform. "We call them the little hands, and you can immediately see their different claws, which lower the quality of the work...".[10]Affirms a stamp service controller. These controllers, check the number of knots, texture, pattern regularity, pattern symmetry, colors and weight of the mat. And it is only at the end of the morning that the mats will be stamped and generally there are no mats refused unless there is a noticeable failure.

Illustration #42: The controller weighs the belt first.

---

[10]Ibidem, p: 22.

Figure 43: The controller takes measurements of the belt with the help of the weavers.

Illustration n°44 : a series of mats for stamping with ONAT

The weavers await the results with anxiety because the price of the carpet will depend on its ranking first or second choice. The second choice reduces the price of the carpet by half.

Then at the carpet souk they follow the crier with a lot of stress hoping to get a good price to be able to pay off their debt from the purchase of the wool and to pay the morning ones so that they do not look for work elsewhere. "Indeed, it is necessary to pay back the wool merchant - a question of confidence - to pay the help of the morning girls, to acquire new raw material, to straighten the loom and to make a new weft[11]. This is what all weavers think about.

In spite of fatigue and stress, weaving is their only way to live, it is their only know-how. But if they find another job with better pay and social security coverage, they will not hesitate to change jobs. This is one of the reasons responsible for the degradation of this sector so important in the economy of our country because it can serve several other sectors such as tourism.

These testimonials implicitly refer to us:

To the theory of the genre that the writer Habib Ben Mansour draws from it in this quotation :

"The Tunisian woman appears here as the unchanging guardian of a tradition, originally domestic and now radiating in the world. In the diversity of their territories, the symbolization of their concerns, women give to all carpets ... their texture, their meaning. From gesture to sign, from carpet to weaving, they are the true artisans of this textile civilization; the hands, often anonymous, which, for centuries, have tirelessly put their work on the loom so that the source of abundance does not dry up[12].

---

[11] Ibidem, p: 23.
[12] Habib Ben Mansour, *op.cit,* P: 13.

II- The contribution of the family in the choice of the weaving loom

These stories lead us to identify several axes: a socio-cultural axis, which presents the reasons why the weavers chose this work sector, another axis which shows the professional career path of these weavers. Each weaver recounts her own experience and gives her point of view according to her individual career path and the personal strategies she has adopted. And we will discuss the professional and personal characteristics that have favoured the change in the living conditions of the craftswomen and their future prospects.

Among these ideological and social axes, as we have pointed out above, we are in a conservative society where man remains pre-eminent.

Among the reasons also of the negation of the activity of the traditional craft industry and thus, the female activity is essentially due to economic choices. The public authorities have turned their backs on traditional craftsmanship, registering it as a subsidiary activity that does not meet the ambition of the main thrusts of the policy of industrializing industry. This unstructured sector, being mostly represented by **housewives, had no trade union defender.** Moreover, it is considered to be "specifically female" work.

Many women continue to work in the **shadows** with very little means without any social protection and with very low pay because they have not chosen to do so but because they are constrained by their social environment and because they do not have other means of subsistence such as a diploma ensuring them a fixed salary in state institutions, or simply by returning to the image of the woman of yesterday as the guardian of traditions.

1- **The family is a main element :**

The family represents a main element in the construction of the personality of the individual, the family framework still holds a determining role in the socialization and integration of women in social life, especially in their decision to choose their future. In the case of the interviewed craftswomen, it seems that, although society has registered a socio-economic and cultural evolution, particularly in the female employment sector, it nevertheless remains conservative in its representations of the status of women in society.

From the interviews conducted, we find that almost all important family decisions, especially those concerning the professional future of girls and women, are still made by the father, older brother or husband. As a result, women often do not have the freedom to express their professional and personal choices. We have noted that the majority of weavers have not freely chosen their professional or even personal future. They are often under the influence of male power. However, it is often for compelling family circumstances, such as poverty, illness or the death of a relative, that Sahelian women turn to weaving as a "refuge" profession.

From these accounts, it appears that family conditions and unfavorable socio-economic conditions are decisive conditions in the choice of this profession, which as we have already noted, represents the appropriate solution for these women to face the difficulties of life since they are mostly illiterate and it is their only know-how.

The precarious family context had very negative and profound repercussions on the construction of the personality of the majority of the women interviewed, such as Madame Mahbouba, who had no choice, her work in weaving being the only way to support herself. Especially as other weavers make their strength from the bad conditions of their family and they set a goal that they must achieve through their know-how like Mrs. Fathia Akoub; the conditions of her family encouraged her to learn weaving and she now has her own project that she is trying to improve even more.

Thus, the family appears in the life trajectories of these craftswomen, as a main and determining factor in their professional career and in their future prospects.

Alliance relationships are also part of the family framework, and can therefore be a considerable asset in the constitution of a working capital for the creation and expansion of a professional project. Mrs. Fathia Akoub thanks to the help of her husband who is also a weaver, and thanks to her relatives who helped her she was able to have a wider clientele and she was able to export her work abroad. Therefore, we can deduce that the family contribution helped her enormously to expand her project and develop her young weavers, "Sabbahat" and to make her creations and weavings known.

Generally illiterate women and those with a low level of education tend to live in a very restricted and conservative environment, where opportunities to forge extra-familial social ties are very rare and almost absent. However, we have noted that some women artisans have managed to have a very interesting social capital to create and maintain the social and professional relationships that are indispensable for their integration into the economic circuit.

We have identified a factor as important as the family environment in the creation and growth of women's projects. It is the construction of an extra-familial social network, which is often informal, made up of neighbors, personal acquaintances, friends and colleagues in the trade, which testifies to the importance of solidarity and mutual aid practices, facilitating the access of these craftswomen to local marketing, for example. Among the weavers interviewed, there are independent craftswomen, who, despite the obstacles encountered in their life paths, were able not only to set up on their own account, but also to change their status, by seeking new niches, both formal and informal.

Mrs. Fathia, after the realization of her own weaving project, tried with her own means to market her productions, through direct contact with the craftsmen of Kairouan.

Other independent weavers, have managed through the construction of a social network to gradually integrate into the circuit of the Kairouanese carpet market. To impose themselves in this field, they had to knock on all the doors and contact several times the people in charge of the craft. They managed to exhibit their products in national and even international fairs.

It is also important to mention that the help of friends or family living abroad is very important, because without them, for example, Mrs. Fathia could not have had any orders from abroad nor would she have been able to try today to maintain an international trade with carpets.

These networks are essential for women artisans who want to develop themselves professionally and improve their living conditions outside the traditional family environment.

2- <u>Social relationships within the family</u> :

Nevertheless, these accounts have enabled us to observe some important changes in gender relations, within the family and in Tunisian society in general, although decision-making power is often held by men. In fact, we note that since independence, gender relations within and outside the family have clearly undergone many changes that have improved the economic contribution of Tunisian women, as evidenced by the evolution of the female labor force. Statistical data show us that the rate of the active female population is evolving.

As a result, this evolution has influenced family life, creating a new framework referring to the pluriactivity of family members regardless of the environment in which they live. In fact, the head of the family is no longer the sole provider of resources as in the past.[13]

It emerges from all the life trajectories of these women, the importance of the family framework not only in the decision of the choice of career path but also in its evolutionary process. These women were all supported by their family environment, through the moral and material assistance of their parents or relatives. Mrs. Fathia Akoube was supported by her father and especially by her aunts who taught her the trade and transferred all their know-how to her, then by her husband.

---

[13]A. Khouaja, mobilité résidentielle, géographique et sociales des familles et des femmes ", in les mutations sociodémographiques de la famille Tunisienne, 2006 Tunis, ONFP, p :102.

We also note that these new family structures that have generated practices of solidarity, aimed at promoting the status of these craftswomen have greatly contributed to the preservation and enhancement of the know-how of Kairouanese weaving. On the other hand, we have noted in recent years the growing interest of operators in the handicraft sector to encourage women artisans to settle for their own account or to develop their projects by encouraging them to access the status of women entrepreneurs.

The life trajectories of the interviewed craftswomen clearly show that despite the precariousness of their living conditions and their low level of education, these weavers have tried throughout their lives to take up the challenge and overcome several obstacles, which hindered their evolution.

In order to do so, they have tried to accumulate several symbolic, material and technical resources in order to progress, both on a personal and professional level. In this way, they have been able to rebuild a positive image of themselves and their role in society.

These weavers have managed to realize their childhood dreams by acquiring an acceptable level of education. Today many of them, apart from those who have encountered many obstacles, are satisfied with what they have achieved and with the improvement of their social level. The qualitative changes in the personalities of these weavers are acquired thanks to their will, determination and desire to assert themselves and succeed.

In order to become even more involved in their professional careers, these weavers have looked for other assets to develop their knowledge. They are still trying to further strengthen their economic and cultural potential by inserting themselves into public and associative life through civil associations, which will be discussed later in the fourth chapter.

By participating in all the political and associative activities of the city, they have managed to get more help and encouragement.

Many of the weavers among those I interviewed are illiterate, or have basic knowledge, not even having finished their primary education, but they do not have so much regret since they are doing a job that they love and through which they participate in the safeguarding of a very rich material and cultural heritage that is unfortunately disappearing.

These weavers just want to acquire other technical skills to facilitate the flow of their carpets and to access markets directly. They are doing their utmost to increase sales opportunities and to look for other marketing niches.

According to the survey conducted, it turns out that these craftswomen are more aware today of their potential and their socio-economic rights. In fact, through a process of self-empowerment and self-assertion, these craftswomen have come a long way, although full of pitfalls, due mainly to the traditional socio-cultural system, still dominant, where resistance to changes in patriarchal mentalities characterizes the majority of our society. However, these women are constantly trying to fight the difficulties that hinder their progress, in order to show their family and professional environment their technical and personal potential and to act on the same footing as men and sometimes better than them.

The analysis of these interviews has shown us the importance of the socio-economic role of women artisans in their family environment and their essential contribution to the dynamics of regional socio-economic development.

To conclude we note that despite the existence of some differences between the professional and personal trajectories of these craftswomen, they all resemble each other, in terms of their deliberate choice to invest more in this profession and their determination to achieve self-empowerment and autonomy. In spite of their modest socio-economic conditions and low or non-existent education, these women have managed to gradually enter economic life and change their lives and those of their families.

III- Women carpet weavers on the fringe of its commercialization

1- Weavers and social perception

Gender" is a sociological concept that takes its sources from the social and cultural relationships established and constructed between men and women and that leads to social attitudes and behaviors in different circles of society regardless of gender. It is therefore a social and cultural classification between masculine and feminine.

If sex refers to the biological difference between men and women, the concept of gender takes these sources of their social differences and their relationship. If physical difference is a constant, gender can be transformed. The main element in this change is the role and responsibility assigned to men and women. They are the result of essentially cultural, social, political and religious factors. They are specific to each society and vary from one gender to another. They always remain a human work

Inequality is manifested in our societies by the non-recognition and under-valuation of women's work: Women's work, because it takes place mostly in the domestic setting, is not recognized at its true value.

While women remain a clear minority in the composite group of non-employees, there are some developments and shifts in the composition of the non-employee group that deserve attention. On the one hand, in declining sectors, such as handicrafts, women are playing an increasing role, whether in formalizing their work in family businesses or in creating more autonomous activities.

On the other hand, women are also participating in the recent revival of self-employment, their presence then following the heterogeneity of independence itself, with the rise of two distinct segments: the liberal professions and self-entrepreneurs. How then can gender relations be rethought in the dynamic framework of the recomposition of independence? In what way are women's positions transformed? Between sociology of employment and work, and in line with the work of sociology of work and gender, one can notice the emergence of new female figures in self-employment and allows us to document the specific forms of investment of women in independence, as well as the changes in gender relations that result from this.

Also new vulnerabilities and the recomposition of generative inequalities. Indeed, it seems that women could particularly suffer from certain aspects of professional independence.

First of all, these activities often still rely on family mobilization, thus replaying the gendered inequalities of domestic and family work, in cases where the enterprise assumes a "common cause" at the household level, even when the women are themselves independent.

Secondly, and more broadly, self-employment is defined by its less statutory regulation, strong internal inequalities, long working hours and a great porosity of professional and domestic spaces and times.

Born and living in a very conservative socio-cultural system governed by heavy male domination in rural and peri-urban areas, many female weavers left school very early, or never went to school at all. The majority of respondents have an educational level that does not exceed grade 6. Thus, these weavers consider this practice not only as a socio-economic activity of proximity, transmitted by family inheritance, but also as a "refuge" solution following their dropping out of school. This justifies the motivation of the majority of these women to get involved very early (between 8 and 12 years old) in the learning of this know-how.

Under pressure from the family, many young girls were forced to stop their studies and go into weaving. This craft is often practiced in the domestic space, or in workshops where they are sheltered from the outside world and far from the company of unappreciated men. According to the weavers, this family tolerance towards the choice of this craft is explained by the fact that the workshop is an exclusively female environment, considered "healthy" and ideal by the families who allow their daughters to go out of the house to work there. Some weavers, declare to have undergone, at the beginning of their departure for work, the control of the family environment and the local society. Other social factors, no less important, guided the choice of weavers to take up this profession, such as the non-existence or distance from schools in rural areas.

Apart from the social conditions, especially family conditions, which are behind the choice of the weaving activity, for some craftswomen, there are other weavers who affirm that their choice is deliberate and without any family constraint.

One of the weavers, whom we met at the National Handicraft Office during the survey, bringing her carpet for stamping, told us about her passion for this weaving craft saying: "When I weave a carpet, I feel like I am painting a picture, I love weaving. That's why I keep on weaving even though it's not so much an altarpiece anymore, in fact I love my work. »

Another weaver spoke enthusiastically about her early love of weaving, saying: "When I was very young, I used to take my mother's place in front of the loom and imitate her discreetly, especially when she was busy with household chores. Up to now, I remember her knocks when she realized that my work was discreet and badly done".

We also quote another who spoke frankly saying: "I never liked school, I only did primary school, I was rather passionate about weaving. In spite of marketing difficulties, unprofitability and fatigue, I always want to do a sophisticated job that meets the standards of first-class stamping, to get a good price".

Through the answers of these weavers, we were able to grasp their attachment and enthusiasm to this traditional know-how. According to the survey carried out, most of the weavers affirmed that handicraft, especially carpet weaving, is a women's work. Because there are many male artisans who make the weaving of scarves and traditional fabrics such as "Hayek".

In fact, it is unfortunate that most people do not see this carpet as a work of art rather than a simple decorative object. On the market, it should compete with a painting, a sculpture, but not with an industrial carpet. These carpets should be signed in order not to go abroad anonymously; the origin should appear there too. It is absolutely necessary to promote our regions culturally and linguistically, to open museums to exhibit our crafts, our art. It would also be necessary to create "*non-governmental organizations in the form of non-profit associations and for the public interest*" which decide to play the role of intermediary between the producers and the market, because most often the carpets are bought and resold by private individuals and the weavers only get one tenth of their final value, even though they have invested time and money in them. They could also create a website to sell them directly themselves. But here the problem of illiteracy comes into play. Rural women are also victims of illiteracy, they don't know how to use medicine to treat their children; all this because some areas are landlocked and don't have access to infrastructure.

2- Women and artistic creation

Our objective is to study the specific difficulties encountered by women in reconciling professional life with family and parental life.

Housewives are statistically classified as inactive women and are therefore not, a priori, concerned by the labor market. However, the relationship of so-called "inactive" women to work and to the labor market is much more complex than the common representations suggest.   In addition to family and parental activities, during their period of life "at home", housewives develop a series of productive, creative and service activities that go beyond the family sphere and which contribute to providing them with a series of social, psychological and symbolic rewards, as well as ensuring them occasional or more regular income. This occasional relationship with productive activities allows them to develop a series of skills of which they are not always aware themselves, whereas they could be mobilized to facilitate their return to the labor market and thus improve their employability.

If they are in fact unemployed, sometimes for long periods of time, our research aims to understand how they manage their return to the labour market.

Analysis of the interviews conducted showed that the relationship to the labor market and the job market of so-called "inactive" women is much more complex, with "step-by-step" folds, occasional and irregular returns, and numerous and varied activities outside the family circle. This leads us to speak of a dotted line relationship to the labor market for these women. Today's housewives are women who are shifting the boundaries of undeclared work, declared work and activities in the home. They are balancing actresses, who share the destiny of many people today, between two statuses, two jobs or two lifestyles. We aim to document these activities which are invisible and rarely translate, for women and those providing support in the labour market, into skills that can be valued in professional careers.

People in today's society define themselves primarily by their professional status, to the point that what we do as a profession becomes by extension what we are, with the result that many identify themselves by naming their profession. We are in a society where housewives are less and less considered.

Numerous studies have highlighted the progressive and continuous increase of women in the labour market.

Housewives are found in both the non-graduate and graduate categories, although proportionately fewer of them are graduates. Our research also shows the multiple attempts to satisfactorily reconcile family and work life and the need to have sufficient income to meet family needs.

There are few studies on the organization of housewives' days and their activities, as if being a "housewife" and being involved in domestic and parental tasks were enough to describe the totality of their daily lives.

Domestic and parental work has long remained "invisible work", little considered by society first of all, but also by the political, economic and scientific world. However, some authors have tried to establish the value of domestic production activities. Generally speaking, all tasks that can be "outsourced" and which can be taken over by a third party have been accounted for, whether they are domestic tasks in the literal sense (laundry, meal preparation, housekeeping, shopping, etc.), or parental tasks (childcare, games, education, carpooling).

We therefore decided to carry out a survey with women who corresponded to our criteria, favouring several avenues: we surveyed several weavers. These women, informed of our interest in this study, agreed to be interviewed about their professional trajectory and their relationship with the job market. We were thus able very quickly to constitute a sample of several women chosen on the basis of criteria ensuring its diversity: criteria of age (in the 30-60 age bracket), intellectual, academic or qualification level, environment (rural, urban or peri-urban), number of years spent at home and family situation (number of children, living in a couple or not). Our objective is to have a sample that represents the diversity of the realities of housewives.

We chose to use a qualitative research methodology, which we felt was the most relevant in order to gain an in-depth understanding of these women's experiences. Our objective was to work on life trajectories and therefore to highlight the professional and family background and the different elements put forward to explain it. This approach seems to us to be the most relevant to give meaning to behaviors, but also to bring out new analytical frameworks and new themes. In fact, the data collected in this way allowed us not only to confirm a whole series of hypotheses formulated a priori, but also to see emerging, thanks to the principles of inductive research, the new elements that are the subject of this research.

We conducted individual interviews in the form of life stories centered on the lives of the women we met. The interviews were conducted face-to-face. They were structured around an identical framework of very broad questions dealing with education, work experience, the period spent at home, the decision and strategies for entering the job market and starting work.

Although the choice of our sample primarily meets this criterion of diversity, we are forced to note that we have few women under 40 years of age and that the sample is composed mostly of women with relatively high degrees. We would also have liked to diversify by origin (by targeting different cultures or migration paths), but our attempts were not conclusive.

We met the women in different places: in their homes, in a handicraft shop, in the national office of handicrafts, in the premises of an association they attend. Each interview lasted between 1 and 2 hours.

The interviews were recorded with the prior consent of the women interviewed and then transcribed in full.

All the housewives we met develop different types of outside activities. In most cases, they do not do them in order to position themselves proactively on the job market, but rather because of other logics of action that we will analyze in the rest of this article. Nevertheless, these different activities are not unrelated to the labour market.

The types of activities identified are as follows:

- Investing in volunteer activities ;

- artistic creation ;

- training ;

- Undeclared, occasional or small-scale work ;

- a process of moving back and forth in the declared labour market.

We will begin by introducing these different types of activities, explaining which tasks they correspond to and why housewives do them. We will also highlight the effects of this investment on them (especially their sense of recognition), on their families and on their environment. Next, we will present the logics of action underlying these activities, logics of action that are largely similar to those underlying paid activities. Finally, these action logics are related to different contextual variables.

This step is important because it allows us to take into account the heterogeneity of housewives' profiles and therefore the skills they have to offer on the labour market as well as the diversity of trajectories: there is no one way to be a "housewife". We will conclude by making the link with the notion of employability and the question of how the skills developed in this way can be valued on the labour market.

Artistic creation: An opportunity for economic development

Artistic creation can take very different forms depending on the cases encountered. This creation concerns among others the weaving of carpets. These activities are not the exclusive prerogative of women living in a privileged environment, even if the most recognized arts are mainly found among women with the highest academic levels (a woman sculptor, women painters, women musicians, women jewelry creators). Through this creation, women seek to "produce" works and objects that are recognized, to create an identity other than that of a housewife.

They are strongly linked to a moment of personal pleasure. It is quite remarkable that they almost always present these activities as an accessory and do not interfere with family life.

Moreover, even when the artistic occupation fills 6 to 8 hours of their days or when it leads to exhibitions, performances and sales, these women do not recognize themselves as artists.

Perhaps we are dealing here with a generated definition of who we are and what we do. This recognized definition, according to which a woman who devotes a few hours every day to weaving, or to any other activity, while assuming the daily management of the home, describes herself above all as a housewife who has an accessory and leisure activity.

Some of them aspire to use these occasional activities as a springboard to a new status; that of independence. Our research on women's entrepreneurship has shown that many women start their businesses in crafts and other creative commercial activities that were an extension of a home-based activity developed during a period spent at home. For some of them, this would be an opportunity to return to the labor market, but many will face the challenge of transforming this leisure activity into a profitable one.

Training: anticipating the return to the job market

Part of the free time is used by some to engage in training, more or less long. They make this choice either out of personal interest, to better manage their family situation, or with a view to returning to the job market at a later date. These training courses may last a few days or several years, and may be more or less restrictive in terms of schedules, working from home, internships and exams. The greater the investment, the more family support plays a role in the continuation of the training. Indeed, some training courses meet requirements similar to those of a job.

Commitment to this approach will therefore depend on the age and number of children, the support of the spouse, and the help available in the local network. It sometimes makes it possible to set up a new distribution of roles within the couple.

Nevertheless, some women continue to be responsible for everything, for example, preparing meals in advance so that the spouse and children only have to heat them up.

These trainings are presented as a need by the women we met because it gives them an opening to the outside of the household and generally gives them renewed self-confidence. They also have a positive effect on the way they are viewed by their relatives, especially their children.

Casual work: having money "of your own".

Among modest households, the development of occasional paid activities is born of the desire to "put butter in the spinach" or to be able to "spoil the children" by improving daily life.

There is also a lack of recognition of women's work in the household by the husband and thus a willingness to prove to him that they are capable of contributing to the household income as well.

For some, the challenge is to finance some of their personal needs. The women we met rarely asked themselves the question of their personal financial autonomy at the time of retirement. On the other hand, this question appeared in all the interviewees as soon as they wanted to develop activities "for them".

Tensions in the couple also push women to seek to guarantee a minimum of financial autonomy and to anticipate a possible return to the job market in the event of separation or widowhood.

The women who generally do not have a diploma prefer to do handicraft work such as weaving at home, with a boss or in a craft industry as workers, although there are some of them who master the weaving know-how rather than cleaning the houses of acquaintances or neighbors, work that is not well regarded in our society or work a few hours in the restaurant sector. The home sale of these handcrafted creations is an activity that can be found in different social categories. These are the creative activities mentioned above, but this time they are partially transformed into a commercial activity, most often undeclared; they therefore do not lead to any status.

When they are declared, it is sometimes in the name of the husband who takes on a complementary self-employed status, a status that women cannot take on because they are unemployed and/or receiving unemployment benefits.

This situation confirms the idea put forward that female activity in the traditional handicraft sector is in the informal sector. For this working population is not recognized as such because it has not yet benefited from the various provisions of legislation concerning the craft in general and traditional crafts in particular. It may be necessary to wait and give time to new structures such as non-governmental organizations and civil associations that are responsible for overseeing the craft activity, the census of artisans and the organization of trades. But while waiting for the effective assumption of responsibility for this sector and especially the female activity which remains marginalized until now, what is the situation on the ground?

For some of them, it is a way of testing the opportunity to make a commercial activity out of it, with a complementary or principal self-employed status "a little later".

However, while many of the women interviewed had considered going into self-employment, very few had taken the step out of fear of the costs and procedures associated with the status and investment involved. Undeclared work is paradoxically perceived as less risky.

These occasional activities, in addition to their financial contribution, are often presented as an opening to the outside world. They often choose occasional paid activities in which they find pleasure and recognition that give them a sense of social usefulness and allow them to maintain a social life. These activities also contribute to giving them an "active" identity with their loved ones and in their own eyes. These activities are subject to an imperative and striking condition: they must not interfere with family organization. They are organized in the areas of freedom: during school time or in the evening, when the children are in bed and parental and family tasks are taken care of. They choose activities where they can have a certain autonomy in the management of their work schedule and, to a certain extent, the conditions in which they work. This result shows that undeclared work, in addition to the exploitation and insecurity associated with it, makes it possible to escape from certain aspects of the wage condition and that it sometimes joins the old dreams of worker autonomy and liberated work. For example, the worker is not subject to a restrictive work schedule.

Return trips to the formal labor market:

Financial needs are sometimes more acute, so the desire to work becomes more compelling. Women then look for solutions to return to the labour market, but the least qualified are confronted with job offers that are precarious or not adapted to their family life. From odd jobs to odd jobs, they may end up returning to undeclared casual work, perceived as having fewer constraints and leaving more autonomy. (Sabbahat), "the morning ones".

Many of these returns end in failure: difficulties in reconciling work and family obligations, transportation problems, family accidents, precarious contracts, unfavorable working conditions that make them reluctant to apply for a new job.

These return trips enable the women concerned to stay in touch with the labor market, maintain skills and retain a series of rights, including the right to an income.

But we have the impression that it is rather a constraint than a choice. Some also encounter real difficulties to get back to the rhythm of a job and its constraints, the comings and goings are a sign of these difficulties and uneasiness.

We see that these women have difficulty developing a professional project, partly because family realities continue to prevail, but also because the job market is marked by the precariousness of which they are victims.

3- The analysis of the choice of the weaving activity:

We have listed different external activities carried out by the housewives. It is now a matter of following a comprehensive approach to shed light on the rationales behind the implementation of these activities (comprehensive approach). These rationales for action depend not only on the actors but also on the context that structures the behavior, through objective and subjective constraints.

Multiple objectives, creative action:

Some of the women interviewed expressed the willingness to "do things" that have an added value, that demonstrate personal talent, skills and work, "we cite as an example: Ms. Fathia Akoub, who is a weaver and a boss, whose testimony will be reported later". This includes all craft and artistic activities, but also some of the more traditional occasional activities (selling, but in an original way by organizing parades or exhibitions at home, for example, or by creating a website or at international fairs or even through export). Here we feel a desire for recognition beyond the role of mother and wife. A logic of action of personal pleasure, of self-realization (of "time to oneself and for oneself").

A housewife's day is strongly oriented towards service to others: the family but also grandparents, the neighborhood, parents of other working children. Many people express the desire to have time "for oneself and to oneself", outside the logic of service to others. This translates into all creative activities but also volunteering, political commitment, training.

We also feel in some interviews that if this time is desired, women only allow themselves this time under certain conditions: that it does not disrupt family and parental life, that it does not burden the household income.

Many of the women interviewed do not feel sufficiently integrated socially through their family and friendships. The fact of following training courses and developing a semi-professional activity allows them to break out of a certain isolation and become part of networks. This search for contact is done with an affective and social logic and sometimes with the idea of maintaining or creating contacts that can facilitate the return to the job market.

This logic reveals a concern to make oneself "useful" to society by carrying out help and support activities beyond the home. Mere "devotion" to the family is not considered sufficient in the eyes of many women, who do not find sufficient value in domestic work.

This logic is mainly found in the pursuit of training, but also through the exercise of occasional qualifying activities and desired return trips to the job market, by updating knowledge in the field of initial training or in the sector of a previous professional activity, by a creative or craft investment for professional purposes. This logic of action is the closest to a strategy aimed at returning to the labor market.

It is a question, by the developed activity, of ensuring complementary income to the family or to personally remunerate its personal expenses. In this case, there is not always "objective" financial pressure, but subjectively, the woman does not want to "owe" her husband the financing of her leisure activities or does not want to take this share from the household income, thus indicating in a way that she does not recognize sufficient financial value in the work she does in the household to be able to make a personal profit from it. We can thus see that women: seek social contacts, "make-create", "enrich themselves personally", "serve-aid".

We deliberately sought to delimit a heterogeneous sample of female weavers.

Living conditions also play a role. The least qualified women are those who will try to find paid activities to increase their family's overall income (rather than for their personal needs) or to put forward these logics of survival and income level when the couple is in crisis and they are or have been separated.

The separation of the couple often puts women in action and pushes them to invest in new activities: professional training, search for paid activities. They all also emphasize the importance of thinking about themselves "now" and not only about others. Some take advantage of crises in the couple to obtain a rebalancing of the different activities and a new sharing of domestic and parental tasks with almost always the obtaining of a "time for oneself", not negotiated a few years earlier.

The number of children, their age, the age gap between children are all elements that will play an important role in the investment of women in the home because they will determine the time that women can devote to their work. The burden of caring for young children (before entering primary school) hinders women in relation to different activities.

However, we were able to observe that the mothers of large families "let go" of the ballast in relation to their younger children: where they had forbidden themselves from outside activities with their elders, they will allow themselves to do so with the next child, as soon as the latter enters kindergarten (or even before). Indeed, having acquired with experience a certain serenity with regard to the management of their time away from home in relation to their children, they can afford to spend a longer period of time outside their homes.

Our survey focused on weavers who want to work. What is most striking at the end of the interviews is the little mobilization in the job search, by the women and their companions, of the skills acquired during their period of unemployment. Yet it is clear that these activities were likely to be valued in the form of personal skills and adaptability that could be mobilized for job search. It is a bit as if the only skills that were valued were parental and family tasks with, for some weavers, an almost predetermined return to local service jobs (cleaning and factory work).

The interviews highlighted the difficulty of highlighting these acquired skills.

This difficulty is in fact twofold: on the one hand, women themselves are not aware that their skills can be valued on the job market, because the activities that enabled them to acquire these skills are not officially recognized or accounted for.

This could be articulated around different axes:

- Skills mobilized in the sphere of occasional activities: often sales techniques, Internet sales, site creation.

- Skills mobilized in the sphere of creative activities: artistic activities.

Taking stock of these skills and proposing, at least for some of them, validation mechanisms that would allow them to undertake additional training in a "light" way would constitute a significant springboard to employment.

The "weavers" we met did not have this status as a life project and did not want to keep it. Beyond the many activities they carry out "at home", these women, who are classified as "inactive" with regard to the job market, invest themselves during their period of withdrawal from the job market. They also develop artistic activities, serve others or even produce goods and services.

In the meantime, women are dumped into the category of the inactive population: the inactive population consists of children under 6 years of age, the school population, housewives, the infirm, pensioners and other inactive people. Women are only mothers and wives and are overwhelmingly assigned to the shadows of the home. This already presents a first process of marginalization linked to gender and the second process of repression is linked to the nature of the work (agricultural or artisanal).

The problem of women's occupation in the handicraft sector is difficult to grasp because of its complementary aspect to household activities.

Can they be considered as homeworkers?

Home-based work includes a wide variety of activities: traditional activities, in the sense that they are an extension of domestic and cultural know-how: culinary preparation embroidery, tapestry work, etc., and new activities related to domestic work: sewing classes, childcare or not related to domestic work: typing work home repairs, etc.....

This definition demonstrates the lack of rigor in the qualification of work at home.

It should be noted that the craft activity can take several forms: Production crafts, service crafts, traditional and popular crafts and arts and crafts. But we will limit ourselves to the traditional and popular handicrafts that address the largest number of female labor.

Traditional and popular craftsmanship can be defined by the reproduction of ancient patterns by the repetitive nature of the representations and techniques by the use of simple means involving manual labor, the result of the accumulation of know-how is at once, culture, heritage and current production.

In other words, women "weavers" known as "homemakers" are far from being "inactive", but they are, on the contrary, extremely active in the private sphere of course, but also in the social sphere and in a sphere that we could call "para-professional", which our research has helped to uncover.

The contacts and bridges exist and the borders are porous: housewives carry out occasional, quasi-independent activities, go back and forth in the job market. In addition, the activities they develop are crossed by logics of action that are also those found in the world of work. It is therefore important to make these various little-known activities visible and to enable those who have developed them to enhance their value on the job market.

This valorization process will benefit both the weavers concerned and their families and the companies looking for people with useful skills.

This ignorance of women's activity in the traditional handicraft sector is the very negation of women as real economic agents. We cite as an example the situation of carpets which has disappeared from some regions, while we were exporters of carpets by millions of m^2. By hiding the female activity and especially those in the homes we have lost tens of hundreds of thousands of women because they no longer want to work and have lost interest in craftsmanship which has resulted in the disappearance of many trades and income. In addition to this, we have been anxious to proletarianize women's activity in a society where women are the guardians of traditions.

More Books!

I want morebooks!

Buy your books fast and straightforward online - at one of world's fastest growing online book stores! Environmentally sound due to Print-on-Demand technologies.

Buy your books online at
www.morebooks.shop

Kaufen Sie Ihre Bücher schnell und unkompliziert online – auf einer der am schnellsten wachsenden Buchhandelsplattformen weltweit! Dank Print-On-Demand umwelt- und ressourcenschonend produzi ert.

Bücher schneller online kaufen
www.morebooks.shop

KS OmniScriptum Publishing
Brivibas gatve 197
LV-1039 Riga, Latvia
Telefax: +371 686 204 55

info@omniscriptum.com
www.omniscriptum.com

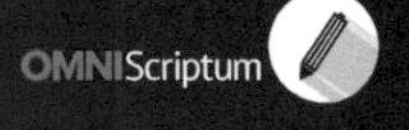

Printed by Books on Demand GmbH, Norderstedt / Germany